D1371809

PLANE CRASHES

By Beryl Frank

BELL PUBLISHING COMPANY
New York

Thanks to the following persons who helped the author in the preparation of this book:

To Vince Mele and Elma Masut of Wide World Photos, Inc.
To patient librarians wherever they may be
To Editor Ruth Cogley
And of course, as always, to Lou.

All photographs courtesy Wide World Photos, unless otherwise specified.

Copyright © MCMLXXXI by Ottenheimer Publishers, Inc.
Library of Congress Catalog Card Number: 80-70570
All rights reserved.
This edition is published by Bell Publishing Company,
A Division of Crown Publishers, Inc.
a b c d e f g h
Published under arrangement with Ottenheimer Publishers, Inc.
Printed in the United States of America.

TABLE OF CONTENTS

INTRODUCTION

The history of aviation in the 20th century would be incomplete without recording the air disasters which have occurred to date. However, statistics show that the annual number of deaths resulting from plane crashes is far less than those recorded for automobiles. But air disasters make headlines. The ones included here were all newsworthy items when they occurred.

The use of the words "greatest" and "worst" are poor choices when referring to air disasters. The growth of the aviation industry must be taken into account. What was once thought to have been the greatest number of people killed in a single plane crash in 1950 would diminish when compared to a two-plane collision in the 1970s. As airplanes have come to carry more passengers, the loss of lives in a crash is bound to be higher. If interplanetary travel becomes commonplace in the 21st century, the disasters which we now consider the "worst" may seem to be minor by comparison in the future.

The number of people reported to have died in the larger aircraft disasters can vary. Immediate newspaper accounts, based on facts at the time of the crash, are sometimes incorrect as to the death toll. Often, survivors of the actual crash die later as a result of their injuries.

Wherever possible, crash statistics have been taken from the records of the National Transportation Safety Board. However, these statistics are only available on United States aircraft. Foreign air disasters are not included.

To ensure maximum accuracy of facts in this book, several sources were used for each crash listed. Where the number of fatalities differed, the numbers used were checked and found in at least two sources.

This book is not a continued series. Each of the 40 plane crashes listed here is a complete story in itself. No single plane crash is like any other, despite the fact that death plays a continuous role in each of the crashes described here. While a plane crash makes headlines, the safe arrival of millions of air passengers is taken for granted. However, the stories told here reflect the pain and sadness which occasionally occur in any growing industry. Aviation safety measures continue to be improved, and attempts are made to decrease and prevent the kind of air disasters which occurred in the 20th century.

R101:   LUXURY VS SAFETY

October 5, 1930

The *R101* was to be Britain's claim to fame in long-distance travel. The luxuriously-appointed airship, which was to make its maiden voyage to India by way of Egypt, included Air Minister Lord Thompson among its passengers for this momentous flight.

The burnt and charred framework was all that remained of the *R101*, the British airship which claimed to be the largest in the world. The airship crashed in the vicinity of Beauvais, France.

Prior to embarkation, the *R101* had undergone some rather severe structural alterations. The ship had actually been cut in half to insert an extra bay. There was no test flight, though, after the bay had been installed and the ship reconstructed.

The fittings of the airship were elegant—silver cutlery, potted palms and heavy Axminster carpeting all around. Travel in the *R101* was to be an exciting affair.

On the evening of October 4, at Cardington, England, 54 persons (including the six passengers) prepared for takeoff. Among these were Sir Sefton Brancker, Director of Civil Aviation at the Ministry, and Lord Thompson, the Air Minister.

Although the airship burst into flames after it exploded, the British flag was only partially burned.

The airship left her moorings at Cardington at 6:36 p.m. with those aboard relaxed and prepared to enjoy a long, comfortable flight.

Shortly before 2 a.m., the ship had crossed the English Channel. Routine wireless messages were sent back to London reporting that all was well. After 2:07 a.m., there were no more messages from the *R101*.

Almost a minute later, people in the vicinity of Beauvais were awakened by a loud noise and a fiery light streaking across the sky. The *R101* had gone down, exploded and burst into huge sheets of flame.

Of the 54 persons on board, only seven were lucky enough to survive. Here, bodies of the victims are being transported from the wreckage.

Of the 54 persons on board, only seven survived. Lord Thompson, who had been so certain that the *R101* would bring glory to Britain, died in the explosion.

This tragedy marked the end of Britain's attempts to launch large, lighter-than-air airships. The great dirigibles which were once the rulers of the sky were quickly becoming extinct.

The dead were brought back to England for burial in a common grave at Cardington.

Blame for the failure of the *R101* was placed on public policy. Had there not been pressure on Lord Thompson for that October 4 takeoff, it is possible that improvements of the great ship might have been more carefully made. In fact, the whole history of the airship might have gone in another direction.

Experts, who flew to the scene after the crash of the airship, claimed that the great structure of the *R101* had actually split apart. The twisted, burned-out remains of the airship marked the end of Britain's attempts to fly lighter-than-air airships.

USS AKRON

April 4, 1933

The U.S.S. *Akron*, the largest airship in the world at that time, measured 785 feet long and carried over 6,750,000 cubic feet of helium. Its history from the time of its christening in 1931 made it appear to some as a jinxed ship.

A misunderstood order may have been the reason that the U.S.S. *Akron* crashed into the sea, killing all but three of the men on board. Here, a section of the wreckage is shown being hauled out of the ocean.

While under construction, there was an attempt at sabotage. At completion, the *Akron* was ten percent heavier than the original specifications. However, it still took to the air as a navy dirigible.

An accident on the ground at Lakehurst, New Jersey, did severe damage to the *Akron* in 1932, and it had to be repaired before further flights could take place. Still later that year, a landing accident near San Diego took two lives.

The press roared its disapproval of the *Akron*, but Rear Admiral William A. Moffet, the father of the American airship program, did not agree. Moffet, along with 76 other men, was on board the *Akron* on April 4. At 12:30 a.m., the *Akron* was cruising about 25 miles off of Barnegat, New Jersey, at an altitude of 1,600 feet.

Suddenly, air currents hurdled the ship, and the *Akron* dropped to 700 feet before leveling. Before it could regain a safe height, though, it plummeted into the sea.

Rescue ships were only able to locate three survivors. Among those three was Lieutenant Commander Wiley, who later testified before the Board of Inquiry.

A misunderstood order from Captain Frank Carey McCord may have been the reason the

Akron went down. Commander Wiley said that the captain had ordered a shift of 15 degrees in course. However, the *Akron's* course shifted 50 degrees. It was this mistake which made a deathtrap of the *Akron*. However Captain McCord did not live to answer any of the charges which might have been leveled against him.

Much of the ill-fated *Akron* was salvaged, but examination showed only that the ship had broken up on contact with the heavy sea.

The loss of the *Akron* was to be the beginning of the end of American dirigibles. Only its sistership, the *Macon*, was still operable. However, the *Macon* met a watery grave in 1935, killing two crew members.

Chairman Vinson of the House Naval Affairs Committee made the final announcement on the fate of dirigibles in the United States: "You can take it from me, there won't be any more big airships built."

The lighter-than-air airship was a thing of the past in American aviation.

The U.S.S. *Falcon* operated the salvage apparatus which recovered the control cabin, shown here being raised from the deep.

Naval officers examined the remains of the U.S.S. *Akron*. The crash of this airship was another example of the problems with lighter-than-air airships and made them a thing of the past in American aviation.

WILEY POST / WILL ROGERS: LOST IN ALASKA

August 15, 1935

Will Rogers, a native of Oklahoma, was one of the foremost American humorists of his day. He was a radio broadcaster, newspaper columnist, author, and entertainer. His folksy brand of humor endeared him to many people.

Will Rogers and Wiley Post are shown here as they prepared to enter the seaplane which ultimately took them to their deaths. The plane, pictured below, had pontoons instead of wheels for water landings.

Wiley Post earned fame as a pioneer in aviation and made many contributions to this field during his lifetime. Post was also a native of Oklahoma and a good friend of Rogers. Since both men loved air travel, it was only natural that they plan a trip together. They were to travel to the Orient by way of Siberia, covering many miles in flight.

The plane they chose for this trip was a red arctic sky-cruiser with a Lockheed Orion fuselage and a Sirius wing. The wooden wings were covered with fabric. The engine was a Pratt and Whitney radial air-cooled geared Wasp capable of 550 horsepower. The Hamilton standard propeller had three blades and was of the uncontrollable type. Post had the plane equipped with pontoons instead of wheels to enable easy landings on water.

When all was in order, the two friends took off from Seattle, Washington, for a pleasure trip which was actually to be their last flight.

Dense fog caused them to make a forced landing in northern Alaska, about 15 miles from Point Barrow. Among other problems, the fog had also caused them to lose their bearings and they wanted to inquire the way to Point Barrow. At that time, Wiley Post made some mechanical repairs to the plane and attempted to start off again.

Fifteen miles south of Point Barrow, Alaska, the seaplane crashed in shallow water. The accident claimed the lives of Rogers and Post.

The plane rose about 50 feet in the air but then fell in shallow water. Both pilot and passenger were killed instantly. A lone Eskimo hunter was witness to the crash.

The bodies of Will Rogers and Wiley Post were recovered from the wrecked plane, and a shocked world was told what had happened. Aviation lost a leader in its field, but the world lost the joy of a man who made laughing at ourselves seem important.

Will Rogers died in a plane crash at the age of 55. This well-loved debunker of stuffed shirts and fancified ideas died as he would have wished—with his boots on. Those who remember the man still smile when they think of him—the man from Oklahoma who had common horse sense and used it.

The Eskimos shown here carried the bodies of Will Rogers and Wiley Post from the scene of the crash to Point Barrow.

THE HINDENBURG

May 6, 1937

An expectant crowd gathered under clear skies at the Lakehurst Naval Air Station in New Jersey to await the arrival of the 804-foot dirigible, the *Hindenburg*. This was the largest airship ever constructed, and the pride of Germany's Adolph Hitler. It was powered by four diesel engines, and its lifting power came from highly-flammable hydrogen gas.

The German airship *Hindenburg* exploded and broke into flames at the Lakehurst Naval Air Station in New Jersey. A listening world heard the radio announcement by Herbert Morrison—"It's broken into flames . . . ."

The *Hindenburg* was only 75 feet above the ground when the explosion and fire occurred. This tragedy took 36 lives in all. The ground crew can be seen in this picture.

man swastika, burst into flames. The time was 7:23 p.m. Herbert Morrison now told quite a different story to a listening world.

"It's broken into flames . . . Oh this is terrible . . . it is burning, bursting into flames and is falling . . . This is one of the worst catastrophes in the world . . . Oh! It's a terrible sight . . . Oh the humanity . . . ."

The ship was 75 feet above the ground when the fire broke out. The tail of the airship began to sink to the ground and, in a matter of seconds, the fire spread to the rest of the ship.

Miraculously, some people survived by jumping from the *Hindenburg*'s flaming belly to the ground below. The last to jump was Captain Max Pruss, the ship's pilot.

The explosion of the *Hindenburg* took 36 lives in all; 22 crew members, 13 passengers and 1 ground crew member who could not run clear of the falling ship. Although the actual cause of the explosion was never proved, this marked not only the end of the *Hindenburg*, but the end of the zeppelin era as well.

Only the skeleton of the dirigible remained after the fire. The ship had been preparing to dock at the Naval Air Station after its successful trip across the ocean.

Only the wealthy could afford to book passage on the *Hindenburg*. A one-way ticket cost $400, but it was an exciting way to travel. The ship's 25 staterooms were luxuriously appointed, and there was a passenger's dining room and promenade as well—not to mention a lounge with a grand piano. There was even a large ballroom.

At approximately 7 p.m., the *Hindenburg* made a perfect approach to the Lakehurst Naval Air Station. Herbert Morrison, a radio announcer with Station WLS, Chicago, was relaxed in his description of the approaching airship.

Suddenly, everything changed. The tail section of the *Hindenburg*, which bore the Ger-

GABLE LOSES LOMBARD

January 16, 1942

Carole Lombard was one of the most popular movie stars of her day. Her marriage to Clark Gable provided the newspapers with headline copy over and over again. The handsome man and the beautiful blonde were loved by the public both at home and abroad.

Carole Lombard and her mother, Mrs. Elizabeth Peters, arriving in Indianapolis for the bond rally.

Shortly after World War II began, Gable was appointed chairman of the Hollywood Victory Committee. It was he who arranged for his wife to go on a bond-selling tour that would climax in her native Indiana. In Indianapolis, Lombard sold over two million dollars worth of bonds. In her last patriotic speech, she said, "Before I say good-bye to you all — come on — join me in a big cheer — V for Victory!"

At 4 a.m., Lombard and her mother, Mrs. Elizabeth Peters, boarded TWA's Flight 3 at Indianapolis Airport. Although she had been urged to go back to Hollywood by train, Lombard preferred the faster way by air.

"When I get home," Lombard said, "I'll flop into bed and sleep for twelve hours."

Lombard finished her bond-selling tour. To her left is her mother, who accompanied her.

Soldiers prepare to lower the bodies of persons killed in the crash of the TWA airliner. Scattered below the rugged face of the cliff lies the wreckage of the airliner. Carole Lombard and her mother were on board.

There were 20 other passengers aboard the TWA flight bound for Hollywood. All was going very well as the big plane winged its way west. There was a refueling stop in Las Vegas, Nevada, before the plane continued on its way—but not for very long.

For unknown reasons, the plane crashed into the Table Rock Mountains, killing all 22 passengers. The wreckage was scattered below the rugged face of the cliff into which the plane crashed. Since the mountains were snow-covered, the rescue was quite difficult.

Two days passed before the body of Carole Lombard was found and identified. Her remains were placed in a coffin which was taken by train to Forest Lawn Memorial Park in Los Angeles for final interment.

The world joined Clark Gable in grieving the untimely death of Carole Lombard. She was 34 years old when she died and at the height of a glamorous and happy career. Many said that she gave her life for her country since this sad event occurred at the end of a successful bond drive.

Clark Gable, grief-stricken over the death of his wife, Carole Lombard. His grief was shared by many all over the United States.

15

TEST PILOT DISREGARDS ORDERS: 55 DIE

November 1, 1949

The day was clear and bright when Eastern Airlines Flight 537 requested landing instructions at Washington National Airport. The plane, carrying 54 persons, was told to head in on Runway 3.

The front section and wings of Eastern Airlines Flight 537 are shown being raised from the Potomac River after a crash at Washington National Airport.

At the same time, Captain Eric Rios Bridoux, a Bolivian flying ace, had run a test flight on a P-38 fighter plane to ascertain whether he wanted to purchase any for the Bolivian government. Bridoux requested landing instructions at the same time the passenger plane was coming down. Although he was ordered to hold at 5,000 feet, Bridoux did not respond. Instead, the fighter plane came in directly on top of Flight 537.

Witnesses saw the P-38 propellers slash through the passenger plane in a matter of seconds. The larger plane split in two, ultimately killing all 54 persons on board. The injured P-38 then seemed to bounce off the other plane, soar into the sky for a moment and then crash into the Potomac River beyond.

Bridoux was still alive when he was pulled from the water; however, he died shortly after his rescue.

Although ambulances arrived at Washington National Airport from all over the city, there was little to be done. Only one passenger from the Eastern flight was found alive—and she died in the hospital a few hours later.

Navy personnel worked far into the night and well into the next day to salvage the wreckage from this crash. The front section of the airliner dropped into the river, while the tail section landed on the river bank. Although

Lights from the airport could be seen at the crash site, as rescue workers continued their search for bodies.

much of the ship's frame was recovered, no one could explain exactly what had happened.

Since the test pilot died shortly after the crash, he could not explain why he disregarded the orders to hold his pattern at 5,000 feet. Perhaps he misunderstood. Perhaps he never heard.

The pilot of the Eastern Airlines plane *did* have time to hear the controller's orders to turn left and he did indeed swerve the large plane. Unfortunately, there was not time for him to get out of the way of the smaller craft coming from above.

Tragedy occurred at Washington National Airport on the crisp, clear November day. Fifty-five persons died in a crash which no one can fully explain.

The front section of the airliner, here being placed on a barge, dropped into the river after the crash with a small P-38 fighter plane.

VACATION ENDS IN TRAGEDY OF ERRORS

April 11, 1952

Pan American's DC-4 was bound for New York City from San Juan, Puerto Rico, on April 11. There were 69 persons aboard the plane, and the takeoff proceeded according to plan. The plane was airborne only nine minutes and on course over the Atlantic Ocean when one of its engines failed. The plane began to lose altitude rapidly, and the pilot was faced with a decision of either turning back to San Juan or landing on the water. The decision was made to bring the plane down on the water, and a radio report to this effect was sent to the airport at San Juan.

This map shows the takeoff point of San Juan, Puerto Rico where Pan American World Airways DC-4 left land only to crash five miles out over the Atlantic Ocean.

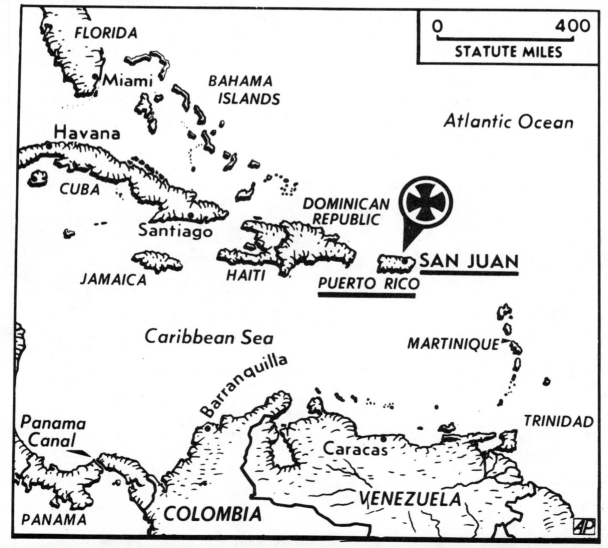

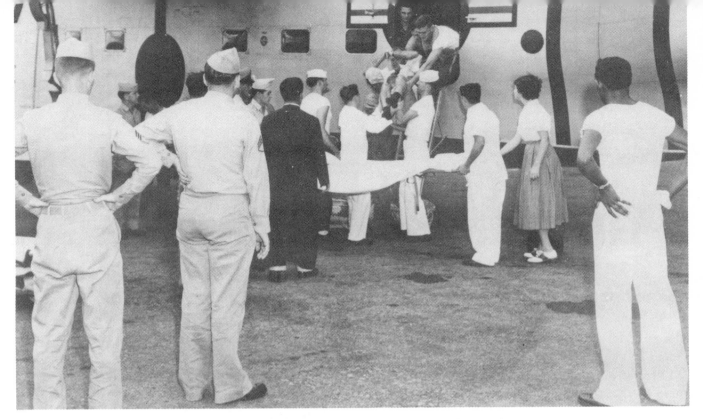

Military personnel from the Coast Guard station at San Juan gave aid to the survivors of the crash.

The plane crashed into a sea of 15-foot waves and here began the tragedy of errors. Members of the crew apparently opened the wrong doors in the effort to get the passengers out. When these doors were opened, the ocean flooded into the plane, thereby hastening its sinking.

Passengers, who had not been informed as to where the life jackets were stored, clamored out of the sinking plane and were forced into the shark-infested waters. Rubber life rafts, stored behind the captain's cabin, were never inflated. In a matter of three minutes after the crash, the DC-4 had sunk into the ocean.

Although the radio transmission did alert ships to the rescue, it took almost an hour before rescue ships could arrive. Those who were pulled from the water had been there for as long as that long hour.

The 17 persons who were rescued from this plane crash were taken to the Coast Guard station at San Juan. There was no help for the 52 others who died.

A tragedy of errors caused the great loss of life. Had the passengers located the life jackets (which were behind each seat of the plane), more might have been saved. Had the rubber rafts been inflated, perhaps fewer lives would have been lost. Unfortunately, neither of these things were done and so, another sad chapter was written in the history of aviation crashes.

Mark Van Daalen, son of Mr. and Mrs. Leo Van Daalen of St. Paul, Minnesota, was taken to a nearby hospital after his rescue at sea. Both of his parents and 50 other passengers died in the crash.

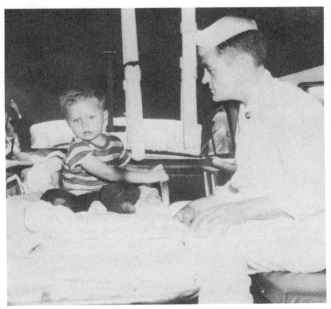

PILOT ERRS— GLOBEMASTER CRASHES

December 20, 1952

There were 131 soldiers and crew members on board the United States Air Force C-124 Globemaster on a cold December day at Larson Air Force Base. The nearest town to the base was Moses Lake, Washington.

The big double-decker plane's preparations for takeoff were normal, and the C-124 taxied down a 10,000-foot runway. Nothing seemed to be wrong with either the pilot or plane.

The tail section of the C-124 Globemaster was the largest piece left intact after the crash at Larson Air Force Base near Moses Lake, Washington.

Within two minutes after takeoff, the huge plane started downward. It took only seconds for the C-124 to crash onto the snow-filled plain at the end of the airstrip. Helpless onlookers saw the plane break up with at least a dozen explosions.

A dispatcher who saw the crash grabbed the nearest field telephone to alert the crash crews who were standing by. Their response was as quick as possible.

The tail section of the fuselage was still intact, and rescuers walked over the flames to pull survivors from the wreckage. There was no way to save bodies from the already incinerated front part of the plane.

This horrible crash resulted in 87 deaths. Of the 44 who did survive, some were scarred for life and all would remember this accident as long as they lived. Pints and pints of blood were used to try to save those who had emerged from the wreckage alive.

Air Force investigators were baffled by the crash when they began looking into the facts. However, the locking gear of the big plane was found undamaged. From this, it was determined that the pilot of the plane had been in error. For some reason, he had neglected to move a knob which would free the rudder and elevators from the plane's locking device. Thus, it was impossible to maneuver the great plane once it was airborne.

The wreckage of the plane was strewn across the runway as a horrible testimony to one man's failure. Had the pilot pulled the correct knob, the crash might never have occurred; and the Christmas of 1952 might have been a very different one for the families of those who died.

Rescuers probe the wreckage, which at first did not yield the cause of the crash. Bodies of dead servicemen lie in the foreground.

This unidentified survivor of the crash at Moses Lake, Washington, is shown being transferred to McChord Air Force Base for further treatment.

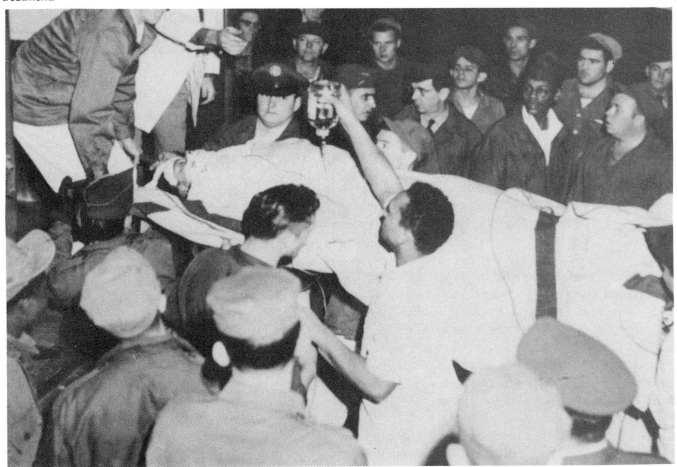

"SALT LAKE! UNITED 718! WE'RE GOING IN!"

June 30, 1956

The National Transportation Safety Board statistics show that 128 persons died when two planes collided in midair over the Grand Canyon. According to one source, the largest human fragment found was "half a woman."

TWA's Flight 2, a Constellation with 70 people aboard, took off about one half hour late from Los Angeles International Airport at 9 a.m. The destination was Kansas City, and the assigned flying altitude was 19,000 feet.

United Airlines Flight 718, a DC-7, left Los Angeles for Chicago three minutes later with an assigned altitude of 21,000 feet. Although the planes were on similar courses, 2,000 feet was supposed to separate them.

When the TWA plane requested permission to climb to 21,000 feet, the air controller at Salt Lake City informed the pilot to remain on course. However, the pilot still asked for permission to climb above the clouds. This permission was granted by the Los Angeles air controller. The scene was set for disaster and death.

The two planes were flying over the Grand Canyon at the same time and at the same altitude. As was common in long flights, both pilots wanted to allow their passengers good views of the Painted Desert. An unexpected thunder cloud obscured the vision of both pilots. The time was 10:30 a.m. The United and TWA planes collided in midair.

The Constellation was ripped apart by the force of the United plane's impact. The plane fell to earth in pieces killing all the passengers and crew members at once. Death was caused by the immediate decompression of air, and the passengers literally never knew what hit them.

The United plane had time to send out just one radio message. The air controller at Salt Lake City heard, "Salt Lake! United 718!

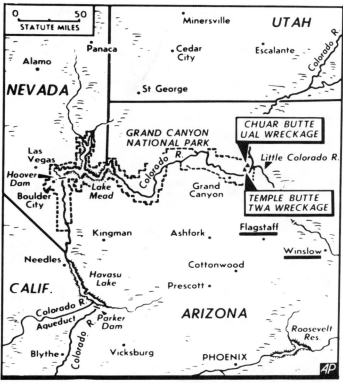

This map shows the scene at the Grand Canyon where the TWA and United flights collided. The TWA wreckage was found in the vicinity of Temple Butte and the United crashed at Chuar Butte.

22

Only charred unidentified remains were recovered from the TWA Constellation. Rescue workers were flown in by helicopter several hours after the crash.

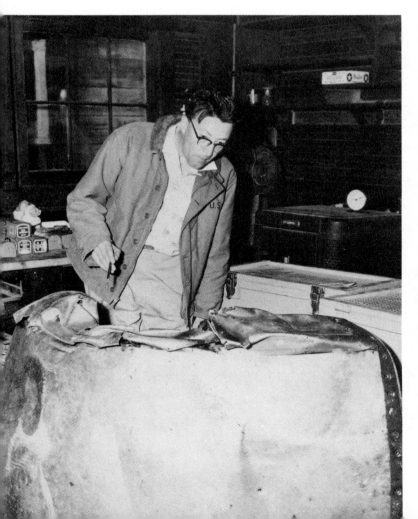

We're going in!" The plane crash dived into Chuar Butte breaking up into pieces as it fell. None of the 58 persons aboard survived the crash.

Rescue planes and helicopters were summoned to the crash scene on the Painted Desert but could not get there for several hours. The sight which met their eyes was gory. There was no living person—just pieces of bodies and pieces of metal from the two planes.

The actual cause of this horrible collision was laid at the door of the air controllers. In 1956, air traffic had increased to such an extent that there were not enough controllers for the number of planes in the air. This was why Los Angeles countermanded the orders from Salt Lake City. Had each plane remained on its own course, this terrible loss of life might not have occurred.

Part of the United Airlines plane was recovered and brought out from the spot where it crashed. Both planes were totally destroyed and all on board were killed.

MIKE TODD AND THE LUCKY LIZ

March 22, 1958

Jack L. Warners, president of Warner Brothers and a close friend of Mike Todd, summed up Todd's untimely death at 47 like this: "The world has lost one of the greatest showmen of our time . . ."

That is how all of Hollywood felt when Mike Todd died, along with three others, in an air crash near Grants, New Mexico. At the time, Todd was on his way to a dinner given by the Friars Club at the Waldorf Astoria in New York.

Mike Todd was best known for his Academy Award winning film, "Around The World In Eighty Days." Although he was a man who made and lost millions, he was considered a genius in the field of show business.

Todd invited writer Art Cohn to accompany him to New York City where Todd was to re-

ceive the "Showman of the Year" award. Cohn was a screenwriter, author, and daily columnist for the *San Francisco EXAMINER*. At the time of the crash, Cohn was writing a biography of Todd titled, "The First Nine Lives of Mike Todd."

Elizabeth Taylor, Todd's famous wife, had originally planned to accompany her husband on the trip. As she was ill with bronchitis, she was unable to go and remained in their Hollywood home in Beverly Hills.

Todd, Cohn, the pilot and co-pilot boarded Todd's private plane in California.

This is the twin-engine Lockheed Lodestar plane owned by Mike Todd, which he named the "Lucky Liz."

A blanket of snow shrouds the desolate remnants of Todd's light plane. The crash occurred southwest of Grants, New Mexico.

The place was somewhere about 35 miles southwest of Grants, New Mexico; the time was about 2 a.m. Todd's plane went down, killing all four on board.

Rescuers called to the scene of the crash found a blanket of snow over the remnants of the plane. The remains of the four who died were taken to nearby Albuquerque, New Mexico.

Aviation experts could only speculate that the fog, snow and thunderstorms which had been reported at Grants on the night of the crash were probably the cause.

Headlines mourned the passing of Mike Todd. Buddy Adler, studio head of Twentieth Century Fox said: "His (Todd's) death is a tremendous loss to motion pictures, not only as a producer but as a man who brought back showmanship and excitement to the movie business."

Two rescuers wrap the remains of one victim's body, as a third rescuer looks away at the scene of the plane crash.

DC-8 COLLIDES WITH TWA JET OVER NYC

December 16, 1960

Trans World Airlines Flight 266 was scheduled to leave Dayton, Ohio, for Manhattan's La Guardia Airport on Friday, December 16. The four-engine propeller plane carried a crew of five and a passenger list of 39. Captain David Wollam advised his passengers that they would reach New York in just over an hour and thirty minutes.

If normal stack up patterns had been followed, the double tragedy of two planes crashing at different sites might have been avoided. No one at the site of either crash realized there was a connection between the two.

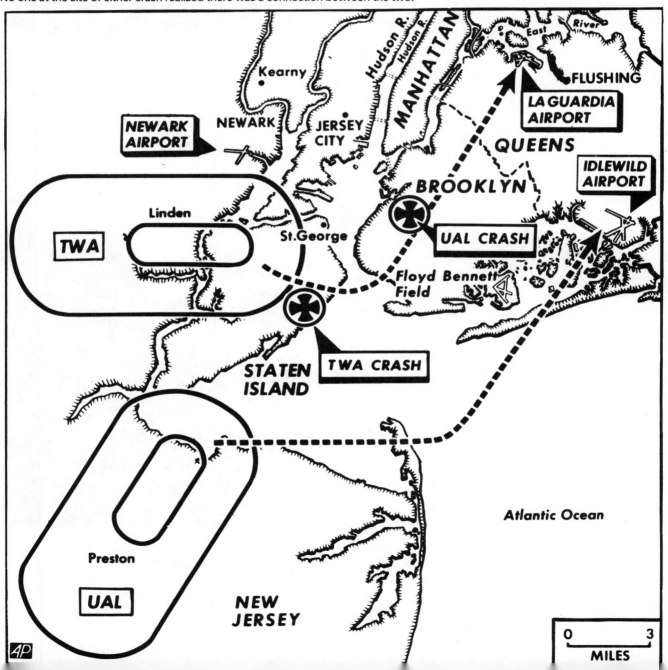

People watched in horror as the tail section of the United Airlines plane fell to the earth on a street in Brooklyn.

Fire Church and destroyed it. A six-story tenement and several shops and offices burned. The fire took more than two hours to control.

All but one of the 83 persons aboard the jet died in the crash. The sole survivor, a child, died the following day.

No one at the site of either wreckage knew that the two crashes were related. However, the men at both control towers watched helplessly as the two planes melted into one image on radar, one falling free of the other and off the screen. A total of 134 persons, including six on the ground in Brooklyn, lost their lives.

Investigators named human error as the cause. The DC-8, not on course, had left its intended approach pattern and, in doing so, ran into the TWA plane.

Emergency equipment and rescue workers rushed to the snow-covered streets to bring help to the living. It took more than two hours for over 250 firemen to control the fires.

On board a United Airlines DC-8 at Chicago's O'Hare Airport were 76 passengers and a crew of seven. This plane, too, was bound for New York—destination Idlewild Airport in Queens.

Both planes were following routine flight patterns. Idlewild (later renamed Kennedy) and La Guardia were monitoring these planes and received constant radio transmissions from them.

Suddenly, the sky began to rain death and terror. The TWA jet started to fall, breaking into three pieces and crashing into an Army base landing field at Staten Island, narrowly missing two schools and several homes.

The Army sent soldiers to the stricken jet, but only five persons were rescued from the downed plane. All of them died before they could reach a hospital. Forty-four persons had lost their lives.

While housewives near the Army field watched the TWA jet fall, a shopkeeper in downtown Brooklyn was experiencing a similar horror. The United Airlines plane crashed and wreckage was scattered over a square mile. The plane crashed directly into the Pillar of

ARMY SAVES $148, LOSES 74 RECRUITS

November 8, 1961

In 1961, it was common practice for the United States Army, as well as other branches of the military, to hire small, nonscheduled air companies to carry military personnel over the continental United States. Although commercial airlines were unhappy with this, the government was still saving money by accepting the lowest bid for air transportation.

Firemen wearing asbestos suits examine the still-burning wreckage of the Imperial Constellation which crashed near Richmond, Virginia, killing 77 persons.

Imperial Airlines was a small firm with a government contract. In 1959, this airline had been fined for using an unworthy C-46, yet the Army continued to use Imperial.

Just a few days before the crash near Richmond, Virginia, the FAA had completed an investigation of Imperial Airlines and declared their safety regulations qualified for troop transport. Until that time, the FAA had been most critical of Imperial.

A nonscheduled Imperial Constellation, an ancient 1946 model, began its flight on November 8 at Newark Airport. Some recruits boarded there and the plane flew on to Wilkes Barre, Pennsylvania, for more recruits. The next stop for recruits was at Baltimore, Maryland. The men were being transported to Fort Jackson near Columbia, South Carolina.

The total number of passengers on board was 74 men. A crew of five piloted the outdated aircraft.

Shortly before the plane reached its final destination, the pilot realized that there was engine trouble. He radioed Byrd Airport at Richmond that engines number 3 and 4 were out. Shortly before 9:30 p.m., he requested and received permission to land at Byrd.

Before the pilot could pass over the airfield, the number 1 engine of the Constellation went out. In a matter of minutes, the plane was out of control. The pilot's attempt to circle the landing strip was to no avail. The big plane lurched downward crashing through a small forest and swamp before it exploded.

Rescuers remove charred bodies from the wreckage of the plane which was carrying 74 Army recruits to Fort Jackson, South Carolina.

Of the 74 passengers and crew of five, only two survivors were able to get out of the wrecked plane. The pilot and flight engineer were able to escape through the cockpit escape hatch. The other 77 persons aboard were reduced to charred and mangled bodies.

The Army drew deserved criticism for employing Imperial Airlines. The reason for using the small nonscheduled flight for air transport was to save money. The money saved on this flight amounted to $2 per ticket. Indeed, the Army saved $148 on the Imperial flight that November day in 1961. Somehow, the country at large did not feel that this saving of dollars was worth the loss of life of 74 young Army recruits.

The airliner exploded as it crashed into the small forest, cutting the trees in half before the final explosion.

ATLANTA'S ELITE MEET TRAGIC END

June 3, 1962

One passenger aboard Air France's 707 jetliner sent a postcard home to her daughter which read, "If I don't come back, don't worry. Don't cry. I will have died happy in Europe."

When the postcard was delivered, the writer had already perished in a crash and explosion which took place near Orly Airport in Paris, France.

Aboard the Boeing 707 and headed for home was almost the complete membership of the Atlanta, Georgia, Art Association. The influtial group of cultural leaders had just completed a trip which included visits to prominent museums and galleries in Europe. They had seen art treasures in the Louvre, the Doge's Palace, St. Mark's, St. Peter's, the Tate and Uffizi galleries.

The Art Association had been responsible for bringing many great collections to Atlanta and making the city a cultural center for the arts.

The loss of so many cultural leaders was a tragedy which some compared to the tragedy of the Civil War.

The passengers and crew on the Boeing 707 consisted of 132 persons. Seatbelts were fastened and the plane taxied to the runway. One observer said later that the plane seemed to be very sluggish in its movements. At 8,000 feet, the plane should have been traveling at 190 miles per hour. The lift-off was a brief rising from the ground followed by a drop to the runway with the nose of the plane headed off the strip.

Those watching saw the pilot throw on the brakes and put the jet engines into reverse. The rapidity of this action may have knocked all of

The Air France Boeing 707 crashed in a small cherry orchard near Orly Airport in Paris, France, killing 130 persons.

Smoke still rose from the crashed plane as rescuers took count of the bodies from the wreckage. The dead were placed in a nearby garden.

the passengers inside the plane unconscious. If that was the case, they never knew what happened to them.

The plane went off of the runway and into a nearby cherry orchard where it exploded. Just before the explosion, the tail section broke free throwing clear the only two survivors of the crash, two French stewardesses who were seated near that tail section.

Police and firemen worked at the scene of the crash removing bodies from the wreckage. It was indeed a grisly task for the living. Word of the tragedy was sent back to Atlanta where families were waiting for the return of their loved ones. The chartered flight, which was to be the end of a grand and glorious trip of sightseeing for the Atlanta Art Association, ended in death upon takeoff in a cherry orchard near Orly Airport in Paris, France.

A charred camera pulled from the remains may have been used by a member of the Atlanta Art Association to take pictures of the many sights his organization had seen before the crash ended the trip in disaster.

FUEL IGNITES, 707 BURNS

December 8, 1963

Lightning, igniting the fuel-air mixture known as JP-4, caused the explosion of Pan American Airlines Boeing 707 near Elkton, Maryland. The crash occurred minutes after 71 passengers had been discharged at Baltimore. The 81 persons who remained on the plane headed for Philadelphia died in the crash.

JP-4, a mixture of "wide-cut gasoline" with kerosene, was widely used by major airlines both in the United States and abroad. The crash in Maryland was one of several more to come which would cause the use of this fuel to be banned for a safer fuel mixture.

It was thought that lightning sheared off the port wing of the Boeing 707 causing the plane to spiral downward and burn in a wooded area near Elkton. The fuel-air mixture in a fuel tank immediately caught fire, and burning wreckage within a 50-yard radius was all that remained for rescuers to find. The fires continued for at least two hours.

As a result of this crash, JP-4 was no longer used for the United States President's fleet of planes. However, it took several more crashes before JP-4 was banned everywhere.

The igniting of the fuel-air mixture in a fuel tank caused the wreckage to burn for at least two hours after the fatal crash.

Eighty-one persons died when a Pan American Boeing 707 was struck by lightning and crashed near Elkton, Maryland.

VACATIONERS FIND DEATH IN THE ALPS

February 29, 1964

Vacationing skiers from London were aboard the British Eagle International flight headed for Innsbruck, Austria. The plane was a four-engined Bristol Britannia carrying 83 persons to their deaths in the Austrian Alps.

Although those at Innsbruck knew that the plane was missing, rescue efforts could not begin until the morning of the following day. Alpine rescue teams found the remains of the plane crushed into the snow and rocks on the side of the mountain. There were no survivors of the crash.

The tail section of the four-engined turboprop, Bristol Britannia, lay crushed in the snow and rocks on the side of Mt. Glungezer near Innsbruck, Austria.

Alpine rescue teams could not approach the wreckage on the day of the crash due to bad weather conditions. When they did locate the plane, there were none alive to save.

The mountains around Innsbruck average 8,000 feet or more and make landing at any time a hazardous experience. On this February day, there was snow falling.

The pilot of the Bristol Britannia had been in touch with the Innsbruck tower when suddenly his signal went dead. It is believed that the plane crashed into Mt. Glungezer and then slid down a gorge between that mountain and its neighbor.

RED BALL OF FIRE: SABOTAGE?

February 8, 1965

Eastern Airlines Flight 663 originated in Boston, Massachusetts and stopped at Kennedy Airport in New York. The flight was ultimately headed for Atlanta, Georgia with several stops en route. The plane was a DC-7B and carried 84 persons including crew and passengers from Kennedy.

Everything seemed normal at 6:20 p.m. on that February night when the plane took off. The flight left Runway 31 at Kennedy, rose into the air and was followed on radar by the radarmen at the airport. Suddenly, the radarman following the plane lost sight of it. There was no blip on the screen to correspond to the flight pattern on which Flight 663 should have been.

Eyewitnesses on the ground later described what they had seen. A housewife said she had seen a "ball of fire fall into the sea" from a window of her home. Still another ground witness described a "red ball of fire about ten feet high above the water . . . I heard a thud, or something that sounded like a small firecracker."

The Eastern Airlines plane crashed into the Atlantic Ocean off Jones Beach a short time

The proposed route of Eastern Airlines Flight 663 was from Boston to Atlanta. The plane crashed into the Atlantic Ocean just off of Jones Beach.

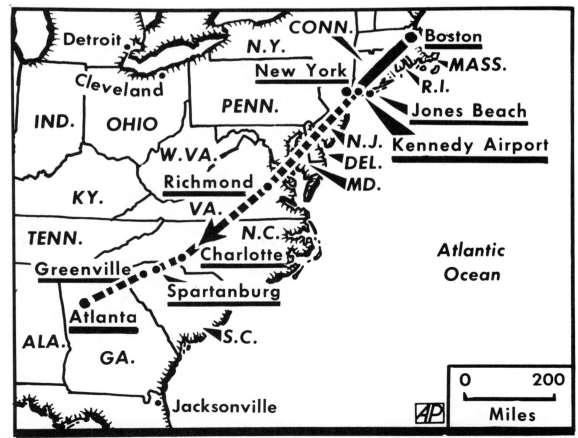

Coast Guard rescue operations found only piles of debris several hours after the crash.

after its takeoff from Kennedy. All who were aboard died in the crash.

No one could explain exactly what had happened to Flight 663. Did the pilot make too sharp a bank to the south and thus lose control of the aircraft? Was possible sabotage an explanation? To this day, no one has definitive answers to these questions.

Coast guard cutters were dispatched to the area where the plane had gone down but it took several hours before they located the oil slick which was floating above the fallen airplane. As the night wore on and the searching continued, debris was pulled out of the ocean.

Parts of the plane were recovered as well as some personal belongings.

No survivors were discovered in the dark night of searching, although several bodies were pulled from the ocean waters.

The Federal Aviation Agency sent inspectors to the area in an attempt to determine the reason for the crash. However, unanswered questions as to the cause of the disaster remained unanswered. No one can say what caused the DC-7B to become a flaming ball of fire and fall into the ocean carrying all of the people aboard.

Here, the dead body of one of the victims was pulled aboard a Coast Guard boat. The rescue operation continued long into the night.

A floating body of one of the 84 victims of the crash was recovered from the water in the early morning hours of February 9th.

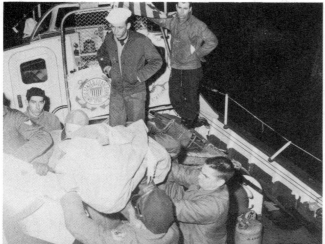

RUNWAY CONDITIONS END MAIDEN FLIGHT

May 20, 1965

Karachi was a seaport in West Pakistan with a population of over one million people. It had once been the capital of the country and was still a thriving active city with a need for air connections with the rest of the world.

Pakistan International Airways was aware of the commercial needs of the people of Karachi and was inaugurating a commercial flight from Karachi with an ultimate destination in London, England. Among the stops planned on the flight was a scheduled landing at Cairo Airport.

The airport at Cairo had received much criticism for its condition before the crash of the Pakistan flight. Approach to the airport was

difficult at any time but even more difficult at night as there were no adequate lights for incoming planes. The crash equipment which the airport owned was not readily available and at times the International Pilots' Association refused to make night landings there.

Conditions at Cairo Airport were poor on the night of May 20, 1965. However, the Pakistan Boeing 720B jetliner was due to touch down, probably for refueling. One hundred twenty

Crushed and broken metal and scattered debris are all that remained of the Pakistan Boeing 720B jetliner which crashed coming in to Cairo Airport.

36

One hundred and twenty-one persons were killed in the crash of the Pakistan plane which had come from Karachi and was ultimately due at London.

seven persons including passengers and crew were on board.

The crash occurred as the big airplane approached Cairo Airport. Something happened in the preparation for landing and the big plane splintered into many pieces.

Miraculously, some of those aboard were saved. One hundred twenty-one people were killed outright in the crash. The inaugural flight from Karachi in West Pakistan to London ended in disaster at Cairo Airport, Egypt.

Although the wreckage of the plane was carefully searched, this crash is another unexplained part of the history of aviation. Was it due to poor conditions in Cairo? Although not proved, this air disaster did accomplish some good. The Cairo Airport did modernize some of its facilities, though they were too late for those who died on the night of May 20.

Pictured here is one who survived the actual crash at Cairo Airport. He was removed from the crash site and taken to the hospital.

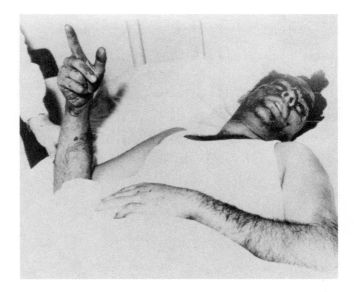

727 PLUNGES INTO TOKYO BAY

February 4, 1966

At 6:59 p.m., the passengers and crew of the All-Nippon Airways Boeing 727 jetliner prepared for landing at Tokyo International Airport. All seat belts were fastened, the weather conditions were clear and the flight was moments away from its completion. Waiting families were preparing to reunite with their loved ones.

Air controllers were following the big jet as it made its airport approach on the radar screen. Suddenly, there was nothing on radar. The plane had disappeared from the screen and those waiting had awful moments to wonder. The plane failed to appear.

For unknown reasons, the All-Nippon jet plunged into Tokyo Bay in flames. Rescue efforts the next day brought up the fuselage from the water filled with dead bodies. All 133 persons on board had died.

Speculation as to the cause of the crash was never proven. Some thought that the equipment had malfunctioned, but from the burned wreckage it could not be ascertained that this was indeed the case. Recovery of the plane never yielded any answers.

Pictured here is the type of All-Nippon Airways Boeing 727 which crashed over Tokyo Bay on the night of February 4.

The fuselage of the wrecked Boeing 727 was raised from the waters of Tokyo Bay. None of the 133 persons aboard the plane survived the crash.

DC-8 BURNS AT TOKYO INTERNATIONAL

March 4, 1966

The Canadian Pacific DC-8 jetliner was en route to Buenos Aires, Argentina, from Hong Kong. A planned stop along the way was to be at Tokyo International Airport, but as the big plane neared the airport, it was evident that heavy fog would force it to circle rather than land immediately. An hour later, word came from the tower that a landing was possible. The fog was thinning out, and the plane could come in by instruments.

Due to the poor flying conditions, when the plane came in for landing, it snagged the approach lights on the field, struck a breakwater wall and lurched wildly down the runway before bursting into flames. Miraculously, eight of the 72 passengers aboard were able to crawl out from the awful wreckage.

According to control tower authorities, the plane had been flying dangerously low.

Although the tower had warned the pilot to raise his altitude, this was not possible, and watchers on the ground helplessly witnessed the crash.

The burned-out wreckage of this plane had still not been cleared away when, on the following day, another crash in Japan made headlines. (See March 5, 1966.)

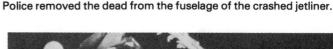
Police removed the dead from the fuselage of the crashed jetliner.

This was the scene at Tokyo International Airport's Runway C on the morning of March 5. The tail section of the DC-8 had been burned out in the crash the night before.

CRASH AT MT. FUJI STUNS JAPAN

March 5, 1966

The weather was bright and sunny on the morning of March 5 at Tokyo International Airport. Airport personnel were still busy clearing away the wreckage of a Canadian Pacific DC-8 which had crashed to the ground during its landing the night before. But that wreckage had already passed into aviation history, and March 5 was another day with more planes ready to take to the skies.

One of those planes preparing for takeoff from Tokyo for London, England, was a BOAC 707 jet. Food cartons for the long flight were loaded aboard the big plane as was the luggage for 124 passengers. All things were proceeding in a normal pattern.

The doors of the plane were closed and seat belt signs turned on in preparation for takeoff.

Passengers prepared themselves to see the great majesty of Mount Fuji.

All seemed to be going well as the giant BOAC 707 lifted off and gained altitude. However, no one had taken into consideration the strong winds which were swirling around Mount Fuji that day. Spectators on the ground saw the plane reach the summit of the moun-

The British 707 jet bound for London is shown here as it was being loaded for takeoff on the morning of March 5. There were 124 passengers on board.

After the plane's crash into Mount Fuji, rescuers covered the bodies which they found on the ground. The jet's explosion occurred while it was airborne.

Shown here are the wheels of the plane as well as the fuselage. Japanese workers sifted through the wreckage searching for the bodies of those who died.

tain and then, suddenly, they saw only smoke. A ball of fire seemed to be exploding in midair; what was left of the 707 scattered over the eastern slopes of the mountain. Pieces of metal which had once been an airplane, as well as parts of the bodies of those within, fell to the ground below.

The cause of this crash which killed all who had been aboard the plane was never determined. Some felt that the BOAC flight had suffered an unexplained midair explosion. To those witnesses on the ground, that was how the horrible sight appeared.

The other possibility was that the swirling winds around Mount Fuji had almost tornado-like force. The jetliner was caught up in those winds and literally ripped apart like a child's toy.

Neither of these explanations was ever proven, though. Parts of the huge airplane and the remains of those who had been aboard were all that could be seen at the crash site.

OFF-COURSE AIRLINER SMASHES INTO TREES

September 1, 1966

Passengers aboard the Britannia Airways plane were British vacationers going to Adriatic resorts. The plane, which had been chartered for this flight, was a four engine turbo-prop Britannia 102 which had begun its flight from Luton Airport outside of London.

Nestled on the ground under the tall fir trees are the remains of the Britannia Airways charter flight. The plane, en route from London to the Adriatic, crashed near Ljubljana, Yugoslavia.

There were 117 persons aboard the plane as it approached Ljubljana Airport in northern Yugoslavia; 97 of those persons failed to reach their destination.

The plane struck some treetops as it approached the airport runway at Brnik Airport. Somehow, the plane rose over the treetops before it crashed to the ground in flames. The time was 11:30 p.m., and the noise of the crash awakened many in the vicinity.

Rescuers immediately made their way to the crash site. Here, they found that some of the passengers had been thrown clear of the wreckage. One rescuer saw three women climb out of the fire and debris, one of whom immediately collapsed and died. The other two, along with others who were thrown clear, were taken to the hospital for treatment.

Twenty-two persons actually made their way out of the burning plane alive. Of these, two died later on as a result of their injuries. Thus, the death toll rose to 97.

According to later investigation of the crash, it was discovered that the pilot was off his course by 110 yards during the landing approach. The pilot was informed of this. How-

This overview of the wreckage shows the worst air disaster in Yugoslavia's aviation history at that time. Ninety-seven persons died in this crash.

ever, for some unknown reason, he did not or was not able to adjust his altitude for a safe landing. This was why the plane sheared off the tops of the trees—which, in turn, caused the chartered flight to crash in flames.

A survivor later described what had happened to himself, his wife and daughter in the crash:

"The plane slowed down," he said. "Then it started to vibrate. A few seconds later, we crashed, bounced back in the air and finally fell down. We were thrown clear with our seats."

This Briton and his family were three of the lucky ones who lived to tell about what had happened on that fateful September day.

PLANE SWERVES, DIVES... ENDS MAJORCA VACATIONS

June 4, 1967

Vacationing Britons had chartered an Argonaut DC-4 from British Midland Airways to bring them from Palma, Majorca, back to England. According to snapshots found, the Britons had enjoyed the Spanish sun and were probably reliving parts of their trip as the plane neared Stockport, England.

There were 84 persons, including passengers and crew, aboard the Argonaut DC-4. Miraculously, 12 of those 84 did survive the crash of the airplane.

As the four-engine plane neared Stockport, it dived low over the city. According to an eye-witness on the ground: "It seemed to swerve, then dive, and then part of it burst into flames."

One account of this disaster states that the airplane hit a power station, fell into a small park and then burst into flames. The plane did indeed crash into the center of the industrial city of Stockport. However, there was no loss of life on the ground from the crash. Since the crash happened where it did, this might be termed an aeronautic miracle.

Firemen, police and other rescuers worked tirelessly at the crash site. Broken luggage, dead bodies and vacation pictures were strewn all around. Although they ultimately found 72 persons dead, there were some survivors to be treated.

The four-engine propeller-driven plane crashed into the center of the industrial city of Stockport, England, en route from a vacation trip to Majorca.

Twelve persons actually lived through the crash. Some of the people who had rushed to the site managed to pull the pilot from his cockpit. The cockpit had been crushed in the plane's impact like a small, broken toy. The pilot was rescued just before the cockpit broke into flames.

One or two of the stewardesses were also pulled from the wreckage. All of the rescuers worked tirelessly to find and care for the few who had survived. The living were taken to nearby hospitals for treatment and, whenever possible, the dead were identified.

All that remained of the Argonaut DC-4 after the crash was the tail section. The holiday trip to the sunny shores of Spain ended in an unexplained air crash at the industrial city of Stockport, England, for most of the vacationers.

The tail section was all that remained intact of the chartered British airliner. Of the 84 persons aboard, only 12 walked away from the crash.

Rescue workers were busy for many hours after the crash which killed 72 persons on board the chartered flight from Palma, Majorca.

COLLISION OF CESSNA AND 727 ENDS IN RAIN OF DEATH

July 19, 1967

The Piedmont Airlines 727 jet was on course after its takeoff from the Asheville-Henderson Airport. The big Boeing 727 airliner was bound from Atlanta, Georgia, to Washington, D.C., and proceeding along normal patterns.

A Piedmont Boeing 727 and a small three-passenger Cessna 310 crashed and went up in black smoke near Hendersonville, North Carolina, on July 19.

Firemen and ambulance workers searched in vain for the living. There were no survivors among the twisted wreckage.

Meanwhile, a twin-engined Cessna 310, carrying a pilot and two businessmen, was instructed by officials from Asheville-Henderson Airport to turn north. Unfortunately, the pilot failed to do this and collided with the forward fuselage of the Piedmont jet. Whether the Cessna's pilot ever heard the orders from the airport will never be known. Only the results can be written down in tragedy.

The collision occurred near Hendersonville, North Carolina. The Cessna vanished in flames as it fell to the ground below, but for a slight moment, the jetliner managed to keep aloft. Then, it too exploded in a mass of black smoke and fell earthwards.

The combined total from both planes was 82 dead. Those who were on the ground found horrible debris raining down from the sky. Bodies and parts of bodies, as well as metal pieces of both planes, came crashing to the earth. A body crashed through the roof of a house, while another fell on a service station's concrete apron. Bodies were hung from tall trees and were later found at many different points in the forests around Hendersonville.

The dead could not answer as to the cause of this crash. The pilot of the Cessna 310 did not live to say why he was off course and in the path of the oncoming Boeing 727. Those who helped in the rescue effort on the ground did not find answers among the grisly wreckage strewn all around. Only the fact of 82 dead in an awful airplane crash is or ever will be known about this crash in the woods of North Carolina.

THIRD DISASTER ON UNSAFE RUNWAY

November 20, 1967

The north-south strip runway at the Greater Cincinnati Airport had been the scene of two bad crashes previous to the one that took place on November 20. In 1961, a DC-4 had crashed there and exploded. In 1965, a Boeing 727 had crashed while making its approach to the runway; fifty-eight persons died in the latter crash.

The actual crash of Trans World Airlines Flight 128 took place in Kentucky just before the big plane was due on Runway 18 at the Greater Cincinnati Airport. The airplane was a U.S. Convair 880 coming from Los Angeles, California, with 82 persons aboard. Although there were snow squalls in the area, there was no apparent reason for any difficulty in landing, according to the men in the control tower.

However, when the pilot began to drop for his landing, he lowered the big plane too quickly. The Convair took off the tops of the trees along the Ohio River and jammed into a fence on the hillside. The plane finally rolled to a stop in an apple orchard and burst into flames. Sixty-four passengers aboard died immediately in the incinerated plane.

Eighteen of those on board managed to get out of the smoke and fire still alive. Rescuers who rushed to the scene found badly burned victims in need of immediate treatment. The quick assistance of those who rushed to the crash site prevented more carnage. However, four more persons were to die after the crash as

The burned-out tail section of the big plane lies in the orchard where it fell.

The demolished fuselage of TWA's Flight 128 is shown here as it lay enmeshed in tree limbs and debris on the hillside approach to the Greater Cincinnati Airport. The actual crash site was across the Ohio River in Kentucky.

a result of their injuries, raising the death toll to 68.

Investigation into the cause of the crash was begun by the Civil Aeronautics Board. The inquiry found no outstanding irregularities. While Cincinnati's electric guide slope indicator had been out of service for more than two months, all pilots were aware of this. They were also aware that Runway 18 was being lengthened.

Despite this report, Ohio's Governor James M. Rhodes did order the runway to be closed down. This was the third bad accident here in a comparatively short time. It was believed that any plane attempting to land here might have trouble from winds and severe buffeting over the hills of Hebron. Since the airport approach from that runway seemed unsafe, it was deemed advisable to close the runway completely.

The safety measures taken after the crash of TWA Flight 128 may have saved other lives at

A fireman sprayed foam on the smoking wreckage of the TWA jet. This was the third crash of a plane coming in on Runway 18 at the Greater Cincinnati Airport.

the Greater Cincinnati Airport, but for those who died on that snowy night in November, it was too little and too late.

Workmen and cranes cleared away the wreckage and debris when the fire was all burned out.

DEATH IN A TEXAS RAINSTORM

May 3, 1968

One account of this air disaster claims that 84 persons died. Another states that the death toll was 85, while still a third source claims 88 persons lost their lives. However, all of the accounts do agree that no one aboard the Braniff International Airlines Electra flight survived the crash.

The Electra was a four-engine turboprop built by Lockheed Aircraft. The plane was introduced by Lockheed in 1959 and recalled in 1960 because of a bad record of crashes. All Electras were studied by Lockheed at a cost of millions, and the early problems with the plane were apparently corrected.

On the night of May 3, 1968, the Braniff Electra was flying from Houston to Dallas, Texas. When the airplane was over Dawson, Texas, it was flying in the midst of heavy rains. Suddenly, the plane burst into flames and fell like a red ball of fire to the ground below. The crash took place about a mile from Dawson,

The smouldering remains of a Braniff International Electra turbojet delayed searchers in the hunt for survivors. There were none to be found.

Stretcher bearers waited in vain at the rain-soaked site of the crash. The explosion probably occurred while the plane was airborne.

The smouldering wreckage was spread over a one-mile area. The plane had been en route from Houston to Dallas when it exploded.

and the people on the ground helplessly witnessed the plane's awful descent.

The smouldering wreckage was spread over a mile of rain-soaked ground. This fact caused later investigators to assume that the plane had actually exploded in the air. Rescue workers had to sift through the charred debris to find the bodies of those who had been on board the airplane. No one survived the crash.

The actual cause of the crash was never ascertained. Lockheed could not explain what had happened. Braniff seemed inclined to believe that the explosion occurred due to poor weather conditions, but this is only speculation.

The known facts are that this turboprop did crash during a rainstorm about one mile from the town of Dawson, Texas. No one who left Houston on the night of May 3 arrived at the ultimate destination of Dallas—another sad chapter in the history of aviation.

SOLO STUDENT FLIGHT KILLS 83

September 9, 1969

The air controller at Weir Cook Airport in Indianapolis, Indiana, had Allegheny Airlines Flight 853 on radar as it approached for a landing. Eighty-two persons were on board the twin-engine DC-9 and there was no reason for anyone, either on the ground or in the air, to fear any type of accident.

Danger from the sky came in the form of a single-engine Piper Cherokee plane. Inside the plane was a student pilot on a solo run. A plumber by profession, this student was making a solo training flight from the same airport where the Allegheny plane was due to arrive for landing.

There was no sign of the small plane on radar control. It certainly was not seen anywhere in the vicinity of the DC-9. The sad

The flight data recorder lies broken amid the wreckage of Allegheny Airlines Flight 853. Eighty-two persons were aboard when a small Piper Cherokee crashed into the plane, shearing off its tail and killing the solo pilot as well as those aboard the larger airplane.

reason for this was that the small plane was not equipped with a transponder. This piece of equipment is a radio or radar set that, upon receiving a designated signal, emits a signal of its own. If the plane was outfitted with a transponder, the air controllers at Weir Cook would have seen that the small Piper Cherokee was in the path of the larger DC-9. The entire accident might have been avoided.

As it was, the Piper Cherokee crashed headlong into the Allegheny DC-9. The point of impact was near the big airplane's tail. Both of the planes fell in a horrible spiral to the ground below, totally out of control.

All of the 82 passengers aboard the Allegheny Airlines flight fell to their deaths near Weir Cook Airport on that September day. The student pilot died as well.

Debris from both aircraft was found in a nearby soybean field. A trailer park just beyond the field also suffered some damage from flying airplane parts and bodies.

Officials from the National Transportation Safety Board, as well as those from Allegheny Airlines, looked into the cause of this air crash. Parts of the damaged planes were taken to Bakalar Air Force Base for the investigation. The conclusion reached was that the crash might have been avoided had the solo plane been equipped with a transponder.

This conclusion, unfortunately, was after the fact. There was no way to change the loss of the two airplanes or the people who died in them.

One of the bodies from the wreckage was hurled across a field and crashed into the side of a mobile home in a nearby trailer park. A part of the body is seen by the trailer steps.

The remains of both planes were taken to Bakalar Air Force Base near Columbus, Indiana, for investigation into the cause of the disaster.

53

MONTSENY MT. CLAIMS COMET JET

July 3, 1970

At 7 p.m., the pilot of a jetliner talked to ground control at Barcelona, Spain. The pilot reported that he was about 12 miles from the airport and flying at an altitude of 6,000 feet. This was the final report heard from the plane.

The jetliner had taken off from Manchester, England, and was planning to land in Barcelona. There were 112 persons on board, most of whom were planning vacations in Spain. The charter flight was a British-made Dan-Air Airlines plane—a Comet jetliner which was never to make its safe landing.

The plane apparently crashed in the Montseny Mountain range near Barcelona shortly after the pilot had spoken to ground control. Later investigations into the crash theorized that the plane had smashed into the 3,936-foot Les Agues mountain. Upon impact, it exploded, killing all who were aboard.

The fuselage of the British Dan-Air Comet was located among fallen trees in the Montseny Mountains the day after it crashed near Barcelona, Spain. There were 112 lives lost.

Although rescuers searched for bodies, none were recovered. It was assumed that the chartered Dan-Air jet exploded after crashing into a mountain.

The people at ground control did not know why the plane fell off of their radar screens. Vacationers who saw the spiraling mass of fire thought the plane had crashed into the sea. However, this was not the case. The wreckage and debris from the airplane were found among the trees in the Montseny Mountains. No bodies were recovered.

This British Comet airliner did not reach its destination. The people who were aboard the chartered flight never arrived at the vacation spots in Spain. The mountainous terrain south of Barcelona was considered responsible for the crash although the actual cause was never fully determined. It was noted, however, that the Comet jet had a long history of fatal air accidents.

Rescue workers had little to find at the site of the final resting place of the Dan-Air Airlines plane—only the broken metal of what had once been a passenger jetliner lay on the ground among the trees. In this case, the wreckage did not give any answers as to what had happened in the air on a clear July evening near Barcelona, Spain.

DC-8 — A MASS OF TWISTED METAL

July 5, 1970

Disagreement in the cockpit of an airplane is an unusual occurrence, particularly when the plane is an Air Canada DC-8 carrying 108 persons. However, an air controller on the ground was aware of problems between the pilot and co-pilot of this plane just before the fatal crash occurred.

The plane was coming in to Toronto International Airport for a landing. The problem which arose was the timing of the deployment of the plane's spoilers—those slats on the wings of the DC-8 which brake the jets while they taxi on landing. The captain preferred to wait to employ the spoilers until touchdown. The co-pilot deployed the spoilers at a height of 60 feet.

Whether the spoilers were the actual cause of the crash was not determined. However, as the plane touched down, an engine on the right

A fireman is shown here hosing down the smouldering wreckage of Air-Canada's DC-8. The plane crashed on landing at Toronto International Airport on the morning of July 5.

Men work through the day amidst the rubble of the crash which took the lives of all 108 persons on board.

The grisly remains of a stewardess' jacket hang from a tree at the crash site.

side of the aircraft fell over, lightening the load by 4,000 pounds and causing the plane to bounce back into the air.

Before the captain of the jet could attempt another landing approach, a second engine on the right side fell off and landed in a clump of nearby trees. This caused the DC-8 to break up into a mass of twisted metal. Huge fragments of the plane were strewn all over the area, some traveling as far as hundreds of yards before coming to rest.

The sudden earthward dive of the plane produced a rain of seats, baggage and bodies mixed with flames and smoke. No one aboard the Air Canada plane survived the crash.

Later investigation into the cause did not provide conclusive answers. Although the tension in the cockpit of the plane was noted on the ground, this may or may not have been the reason for the crash. Could the use of the spoilers have actually caused the two engines to fall off of the aircraft? This controversy was never satisfactorily settled.

The landing at Toronto's International Airport on the morning of July 5 ended tragically for all. After the crash, all that remained to be done was to douse any remaining flames from the debris and clear away the wreckage.

The twisted metal shown here is all that was left when the DC-8 crashed. The cause of the crash was never fully determined.

SABRE JET COLLIDES WITH 727

July 30, 1971

The skies above Morioka were clear on the afternoon of July 30—ideal weather for Japanese Air Force training procedures. Two Air Force F-86 Sabre jets flew in the crowded skies, performing formation turns. Both Sabre jets were without any type of radar and, thus, were unaware of the approach of a large passenger plane.

All-Nippon Flight 58 was returning from the island of Hokkaido with 162 persons on board. The plane had taken off from Chitose Airport, where members of the group had toured shrines of Japan's war dead.

After an uneventful takeoff, the Boeing 727 cruised at about 26,000 feet. As the big plane drew near Morioka, though, the pilot saw an F-86 Sabre jet. There was barely time for the pilot to send out a radio distress signal when the Air Force jet crashed into the larger plane. The impact caused the passenger plane to burst into flames. Debris and broken bodies were scattered for many miles as they fell to earth. Those on the ground saw a white trail of smoke stream over the nearby mountain ranges.

The pilot of the F-86 Sabre jet managed to parachute to the ground before his plane was destroyed, though. He was an Air Force trainee who had been practicing formation turns under the guidance of a superior officer in a smaller plane. Although the instructing officer did see the Boeing 727 approaching, his warning to the trainee was not in time to avoid the crash.

The apprentice airman reached the ground safely—the only person involved in the crash who survived. He stated that he had seen the All-Nippon plane, but there was no time for him to maneuver out of the way. The young man was arrested for involuntary homicide, but, when tried later, he was acquitted.

The white cloud shown in this picture is All-Nippon's Boeing Flight 58 as it fell to earth after colliding with a Japanese Air Force jet near Morioka, Japan.

The wreckage of the Boeing 727 was located in the mountains shortly after the fatal crash which took the lives of all on board.

This air disaster which took the lives of 162 persons was one of the worst in aviation history to that date. Rescuers found parts of the planes and some of the bodies lying in the mountains near Morioka.

Here, a rescue worker climbed on top of the fuselage of the big plane which had collided in mid-air with the Air Force Sabre jet.

Recovered bodies from the crash were taken to Morioka where grieving friends and relatives awaited them.

FOG, RAIN AND EQUIPMENT KILL 111

September 4, 1971

Alaska Airlines Flight 1866 was flying from Anchorage, Alaska, to Seattle, Washington with 111 persons on board. The plane had already made three stops before it approached Juneau on the night of September 4.

According to a report of the National Transportation Safety Board, conditions at Juneau on that night included a low ceiling, fog and rain. The plane, therefore, had to make an instrument landing due to the poor weather. Visibility at the crash site was approximately ¼ mile.

The Juneau Municipal Airport lacked the most important elements needed to bring a plane in by instruments: There was no glide slope device to keep the pilot on the correct approach, and there was no localizer to line up the incoming plane. Both of these were sorely needed on that fatal night.

As the pilot of the Boeing 727 attempted his landing at Juneau, he lost the correct approach. The plane crashed into the side of Mount Fairweather at 11:15 p.m., killing all on board.

Poor weather conditions prevented rescuers from arriving at the crash site for two days. When they did arrive, though, they found only

Much of the wreckage from the plane was small pieces of debris. Rescue workers spent many hours trying to locate the bodies of the 111 persons who died in the crash.

small pieces of the large plane. The jetliner had disintegrated upon impact, and parts of the wreckage were scattered over more than a square mile.

Helicopters were based about 500 yards from the crash site, so they could fly in and hoist up the bodies of those who were found. The dead were then taken to a temporary morgue in Juneau.

One of the causes of this crash was undoubtedly weather conditions at the time. With a low visibility, the pilot was probably not aware of the mountain in his path. The lack of equipment at Juneau certainly further contributed to the problems of the night. Although the causes listed by the National Transportation Safety Board were listed as *probable*, the facts included the loss of life for 111 persons on a foggy night near Juneau, Alaska.

Wreckage from the Alaska Airlines Boeing 727 spread over a square-mile area from the crash site. Poor weather conditions contributed to the cause of the disaster.

Helicopters were unable to get to the crash site for two days to raise the bodies of the dead and carry them to a Juneau morgue.

Slabs were set up at a Juneau mortuary to receive the bodies of the persons who died.

THE "LONG MOUNTAIN" CLAIMS 115

May 5, 1972

Due to the ring of mountains which surrounded it, the Punta Raisi Airport in Palermo, Sicily, was considered to be one of the most dangerous landing fields in Europe. One of these mountains, Montagna Lunga (meaning "Long Mountain") was located just three miles from Palermo. On the night of May 5, an Alitalia Airlines DC-8 jetliner crashed into the side of Montagna Lunga, killing all 115 persons on board.

After the devastating crash, authorities concluded that the pilot had been flying too low. Whether this was the case or not, the results were tragic.

In addition to killing all of the passengers and crew on board the Alitalia flight, the crash caused fires in the mountain's woods which burned for several days.

Rescue workers and national police arrived at the crash site of an Alitalia Airlines DC-8 jetliner. The plane crashed into a mountain near Palermo, Italy.

The morning after the crash, rescue workers located some of the bodies, and the Bishop of Palermo, Monsignor Pappalardo, hastened to the site to bless the dead.

The national police were summoned to the crash site to inspect the ruins of the Alitalia plane. The wreckage and strewn bodies were, indeed, an awesome sight to see.

This flight, which ended in disaster, was considered one of the worst air crashes in the history of Alitalia Airlines. Montagna Lunga had claimed the lives of 115 persons just before they were to arrive at their destination in Sicily.

The dead were laid under cardboard cartons as they were found. The Bishop of Palermo, second from the right, is shown as he blessed the charred bodies of some of the victims.

BRITISH TRIDENT BREAKS IN HALF

June 18, 1972

An increase in the skyjacking of airplanes had caused the threat of a worldwide pilots' strike. Because of this threatened strike, people were anxious to travel before such travel would become impossible. It is no wonder, then, that British European Airways had as many as 118 persons on board.

The jet did take off from Heathrow Airport in London, England, but to the horror of those observers who saw it, the plane crashed into a nearby field.

The body of the aircraft splintered into many pieces on impact, and the tail section snapped off. Only a line of nearby trees stopped the broken fuselage from traveling any further on the ground.

Soldiers and other rescue workers hastened to the scene of the crash. All but two persons on board had already died in the smoking remains

The BEA Trident jet had been bound for Brussels from Heathrow Airport when it crashed about four miles from the takeoff at Heathrow.

The tail section lay among the debris of the fuselage after the crash which caused the deaths of the 118 persons on board the jet.

Shown here are the bodies of victims pulled from the smoking debris which had once been a jetliner.

of the Trident. The two persons who were alive when they were pulled from the wreckage both died before the day had ended.

According to one ground observer, the aircraft seemed to go into a stall after takeoff. Another declared that the cause of the crash was a complete mystery. The jet which had

been bound for Brussels crashed just four miles from Heathrow Airport.

Although the cause of the British European Airways Trident was not definitely established, the remains of the plane showed that the aircraft had broken apart. The tail section was found among the pieces of the fuselage and the fuselage itself was broken. All that remained for the rescuers to do was to remove the bodies of the 118 persons and prepare them for burial.

Ambulances and firemen hastened to the crash site only to find that death had been there before them. Investigators could not definitely uncover the cause of the crash.

DEATH IN THE EVERGLADES

December 29, 1972

December sun-seekers took off happily from New York's Kennedy International Airport for Miami, Florida, and a gala vacation trip. The 174 persons on board consisted of 159 passengers and 15 crew members. The Eastern Airlines L-1011 TriStar was a three-engine Lockheed model, and its pilot had a total of 29,700 flying hours.

The approach pattern to the Miami Airport was clear, and all seemed fairly routine. Radar control scanners at Miami were following the plane, when it suddenly disappeared from the screen. The time was 11:42 p.m.

Later investigation concluded that the TriStar jet had come in too low on its approach. This caused the plane to crash into the swampy terrain of the Everglades, about 17 miles west of its intended destination.

The scattered remains of an Eastern Airlines L-1011 jet lie in the Everglades after the jet crashed into the swampy terrain. The round life raft at lower right of the picture apparently inflated after the crash.

A mud-splattered doll was found among the debris from the plane. Among the passengers were families planning a vacation in the sun. (Photo courtesy of Miami Herald.)

One of the first rescuers to arrive at the scene of the crash said, "The plane is a mess. There are one or two or three large chunks . . . There are little pockets of people. There are bodies spread all around."

Fatalities caused by the crash totaled 99, of whom 94 were passengers and 5 were crew members (including the pilot). Seventy-five persons did manage to crawl out of the wreckage and live.

According to the *New York Times* account of the accident on December 31, one of the survivors described the crash thusly:

"We had gotten the o.k. to land, when the nose of the plane moved up a bit and suddenly there was a crunch. The next thing I knew I could see the sky above me, and I was out in a field holding my briefcase."

Coast Guard, Army and Air Force helicopters rushed to the scene of the crash in the Everglades. Dazed survivors awaited them, and the injured were flown out to nearby hospitals for treatment.

The accident report from the National Transportation Safety Board stated that the probable cause of the crash may have been misread instruments. This might have caused the jetliner to come in too low on its approach to Miami.

The investigator shown here checks the wreckage of the jumbo jet which crashed just before landing at Miami International Airport. (Photo courtesy of Miami Herald.)

Only 75 persons who left Kennedy Airport on that December night reached Miami alive. Those who died perished in an air disaster which has never been fully explained.

Rescuers carried this 10-year-old boy who survived the crash to safety. He was one of 75 persons who lived to tell what had happened. Ninety-nine persons died as a result of an approach to the airport which was too low.

SIX MINUTES OF CONFUSION IN CONTROL TOWER

July 31, 1973

The morning of July 31 was foggy at Logan Airport in Boston. The visibility surrounding the area where Delta Airlines Flight 723 was due to arrive was listed as one mile or less. The DC-9 jet had taken off from Burlington, Vermont, and was on its way to Logan Airport when the crash occurred.

Two airplane construction workers witnessed the jetliner's disappearance in a large ball of flame followed by a cloud of black smoke and a thundering roar. The two men raced to what remained of the airplane and were the only ones at the scene of the crash for

The arrow shows the path of Delta Airlines ill-fated Flight 723. The jet crashed into the seawall at Logan International Airport, Boston.

The dead bodies of two passengers on board were found still strapped to their seats. Both seats had been ripped from the plane and thrown out onto the ground.

Fire utterly destroyed the fuselage of the DC-9, and all that remained was the charred wreckage.

a very long six minutes. The tower control did not know what had happened to Delta's Flight 723. Whether the lapse of those six minutes caused more deaths on the aircraft will never be proved.

When the fire alarm was finally sounded and the emergency vehicles rushed to the scene, they found that death had been there ahead of them. Of the 89 persons on board the jet, only one survived the crash.

The lone survivor had been located by the two construction workers. The man was fully conscious and begging for help. Although he had suffered severe body burns and ultimately lost his legs, he recovered and lived to tell about the crash.

Seven other critically-injured passengers were removed from the burning debris of the airplane and transported to a nearby hospital. Each of these seven survivors died a few hours later as a result of their injuries.

In August, a hearing was held as officials tried to determine the cause of the air disaster. Lawyers from Delta Airlines placed the blame for the accident on understaffed and confused tower personnel. Certainly, the six minutes

which elapsed before the control tower sounded the fire alarm caused a critical delay in sending rescuers to the crash site. Perhaps more people could have been saved had the precious time not gone by.

Still another possible cause of the crash was the malfunction of instruments, as this particular plane had a history of instrument malfunction.

The hearings officer, James W. Kuehl, summed up the results when he stated: "Some crashes are clear-cut from the beginning. We knew this one was a controversial crash and not one that could be pinned down to one cause."

Victims and wreckage were scattered along the runway in this crash which killed 88 persons in the dense fog at Logan Airport.

346 DEAD: DC-10 UNSAFE

March 3, 1974

When the Turkish DC-10, the Turk Hava Yollari, fell from the sky at Ermenonville near Paris, France, it cut a path approximately 3,000 feet long. Trees, parts of the plane, luggage and bodies were strewn over a nine-mile area.

Firemen and rescue parties survey the remains of the Turkish Airlines jumbo jet which crashed at Ermenonville, near Paris.

Rescue teams took more than three hours to reach the crash site, and there was little to do then except begin the gruesome cleanup operation. There were 346 dead.

The reason for this horrible crash was one that may have been totally avoidable. The cargo hatch cover was found seven miles from the plane. Immediate decompression of the plane resulted when this cover came off.

The American team investigating the crash was aware of a similar problem as early as 1972. Then, an American Airlines DC-10 had lost its cargo door and it was only due to superb piloting that that plane was able to land safely.

Although that DC-10 was found to have a faulty locking system, America's Federal Aviation Administration did nothing nor did the jet's manufacturer, McDonnell Douglas. The Turkish DC-10 was built after the 1972 accident with no necessary modifications.

The bodies of the dead were laid out in nearby fields. All 346 persons aboard the jet were killed.

The unusual leaves on the trees were, in reality, clothing of the crash victims.

March 6, three days after 346 persons died in an unnecessary plane crash, the Federal Aviation Administration issued an order to all airlines that ran DC-10's. This order made all necessary changes mandatory. But for the family and friends of the fallen Turkish airliner passengers, that order was too little and far too late.

The international ramifications resulted in a legal battle. Hopefully, that battle will resolve the question of the legal rights of airplane manufacturers, passengers and plane operators. The insurance claims awarded to families of the passengers on that DC-10 were quite large. Perhaps this would insure that future airplanes would fly with the assurance that known mechanical defects would be corrected.

71

ORPHAN MERCY FLIGHT ENDS AS FLIGHT OF DEATH

April 4, 1975

The C5-A Galaxy, the largest plane in the world, loaded precious cargo at Saigon. Tan Son Nhut Airbase was crowded with people in preparation for this particular flight—a flight which was supposed to carry 243 orphans of Vietnam to new homes in the United States. The orphans were cared for by 62 adults. This was to be the beginning of a program to evacuate about 2,000 orphans from the war zones.

The South Vietnamese orphans shown here boarded a giant C5-A Galaxy Air Force transport plane. New homes in the United States were to be found for the 243 children.

When the plane doors closed on the war orphans, children were crowded into every available space, sometimes 10 abreast in seats made to hold three people. Seat belts were fastened where possible and children were strapped down to protect them during the flight.

Minutes after takeoff, the pilot radioed back to the airbase. Something had gone wrong with his rear loading ramp and he had lost control of some parts of the airplane. The only thing to do was to return to Tan Son Nhut.

The giant plane rapidly lost altitude. With only one and a half miles left to reach the runway, the pilot knew he could not make it. Below the plane, instead of the runway, there were rice paddies. The pilot made the decision to put down on the fields below. The plane touched down and skidded across one of the fields. Carried by momentum, it skimmed across a river and finally halted in a second field. The wings of the huge plane snapped off, a fire erupted and the plane broke apart spewing its contents all over the field.

One hundred ninety persons were killed when the C5-A Galaxy landed on the rice paddies in South Vietnam. Most of them were orphaned children who had been on their way to new homes in the United States.

The mercy flight from Saigon ended in a rice paddy 1 ½ miles from the airport. The crash was caused by a faulty rear loading ramp.

Rescue workers could not reach the swampy field by land. Helicopters were used to transport workers to the crash scene and in turn, carry out the wounded to hospitals in Saigon. Bodies and belongings were covered in mud and many of the belongings were children's toys, baby bottles and diapers of the young passengers.

The day which had begun with optimism and hope for the relocation of 243 orphans from South Vietnam ended in death and disaster for many of them. The tragic loss was felt all around the world; these children who died were victims of the war as surely as any soldier who died carrying a gun.

One small victim of the crash was dead when pulled from the wreckage. His body is being placed in a body bag by rescue workers.

The lucky child on the stretcher here lived to reach a Saigon hospital. There were 115 survivors of this awful crash.

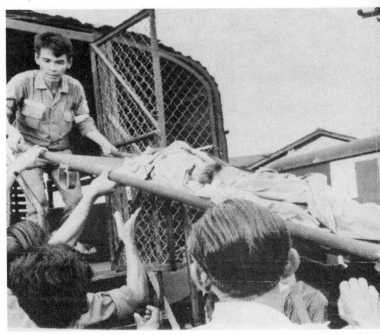

73

NYC BOULEVARD BECOMES AVENUE OF DEATH

June 24, 1975

Eastern Airlines Boeing 727 Flight 66 was arriving at Kennedy Airport a few minutes late. Conditions at Kennedy were wet and rainy but not too bad for landing, and the control tower gave Flight 66 the needed permission to come down.

cars, all dealing with wet streets, burning airplane pieces and oil- and fuel-covered roadways.

One hundred sixteen persons were on board the jet when it crashed. One hundred ten died immediately. Of those who managed to get out of the burning aircraft, two more died of burns in the hospital. Rockaway Boulevard was turned into a morgue in a matter of minutes.

Police and firemen converged at the scene of the wreck. Although the firemen were wearing asbestos suits, the fire moved more swiftly than they did. It took a short time to smother the burning wreck with foam but it was too late for most of the people within. Only a few were taken alive to nearby hospitals.

On June 24, Eastern Airlines Flight 66 crashed at the edge of Rockaway Boulevard near Kennedy Airport in New York City. The death toll reached 112.

None of the people riding on Rockaway Boulevard at 4 o'clock in the afternoon were concerned when they heard a jetliner overhead. This was a common occurrence this close to Kennedy Airport. However, a flash of lightning occurred followed by an immediate crash. The people in nearby cars were well aware that something terrible had happened.

The crash of the huge jet sent burning wreckage all over the road. Drivers tried frantically to avoid the wreckage and other

Policemen view the wreckage of the Eastern Airlines jetliner as a DC-8 prepares to land at Kennedy Airport.

Human remains were laid on the side of the road and covered with white sheets. The heavy rain beat down on those sheets showing that there were young children as well as adults

Bodies of the victims lay under shrouds, as a priest kneels to administer the last rites of the Church.

there on the roadside. There was even an infant's body found which had not been listed on the passenger manifesto.

The investigation which followed the crash of the Boeing 727 was not definitive as to the cause. Since it is an unusual occurrence for lightning to do grave damage to an airplane, this was probably not the cause. Did an unseen wind shear draw the big plane into it causing the crash? The question could not be answered. Did the pilot misjudge his location? Since the pilot died in the crash, there was no way of knowing this either.

The questions raised by the crash of Eastern's Flight 66 will never be answered. All that we know for sure is that the crash carried 112 persons to their deaths, leaving behind grieving relatives and many questions which will never be answered.

Rockaway Boulevard, where this aerial picture was taken, was turned into a morgue in a matter of minutes after the crash.

TENERIFE: WHERE THE GIANTS COLLIDED

March 27, 1977

Although the main airport for the Canary Islands was located at Las Palmas, traffic had been diverted that Sunday afternoon to Los Rodeos Airport at Santa Cruz on Tenerife Island. Los Rodeos was jammed with airplanes and in addition, a fog was causing deteriorating conditions on the ground. There was no ground radar and runway traffic had to be tracked by radio and what the traffic controllers could see. Vision was very limited.

At 1:44 p.m., KLM flight 4805 arrived at Los Rodeos from Amsterdam with 248 aboard. The big Dutch jet was directed to park at the far end of the runway until it was due to continue its flight later that afternoon.

Personal effects, such as a woman's wig and suitcases, littered the ground at the Los Rodeos Airport after a horrible two-plane crash.

The Pan Am flight 1736 from Los Angeles and New York arrived at Los Rodeos at 3:00 p.m. with 378 passengers and 16 crew mem-

KLM flight 4805 was due to continue its course from the Canary Islands at 5 p.m. The fire-blackened wreckage shown here was all that was left of the great plane after the crash.

This was the scene on the runway of Los Rodeos Airport.

bers. This plane was also directed to park at the far end of the runway.

At 5:00 p.m., the runway was badly fogged in. The air traffic controller's plan was to hold the KLM until after the Pan Am was reported clear of the runway. No one realized that both jets were on the same runway.

Perhaps the Dutch captain did not hear the tower instructions to stand by. Undoubtedly, he did not know that the Pan Am flight had not left the runway. The two planes started off at opposite points of the runway for takeoff.

The KLM crashed into the Pan Am at midship as the Pan Am pilot had swerved to the left. The top of the Pan Am jet was cut off immediately, causing a fire in the first class lounge. The KLM bounced off of the contact along the runway and exploded about 500 yards away, killing instantly all of the 248 persons on board.

The total dead from both planes numbered 580. The runway at Los Rodeos was covered with broken fragments of the two airplanes as well as personal belongings and assorted other rubble and debris. It was a horrible sight.

The three countries involved—Spain, Holland, and the United States—all held investigations but nothing could actually be proved. Law suits and settlements mounted into the hundreds of millions of dollars.

Of all the facts known, perhaps the saddest is that this terrible crash happened on the ground. A foggy, misty afternoon in a small airport without ground radar brought about the unexpected deaths of 580 persons. Their holiday trips ended in death.

Scattered wreckage of both planes could be seen from the airport control tower after the fog lifted.

Bodies of unidentified victims of the Canary Islands crash were lined up in concrete vaults for a mass memorial service in Westminster, California. The collision of the two jumbo jets caused 580 people to end their holiday trips in death.

DC-10'S GROUNDED AFTER 272 DIE

May 25, 1979

American Airlines flight 191 was to be a four-hour non-stop flight to Los Angeles. Two hundred and fifty eight passengers and 14 crew members prepared for takeoff at 3 p.m. on a clear, sunny Friday afternoon at Chicago's O'Hare Airport. The fated plane, a McDonnell Douglas DC-10, had arrived at O'Hare a few hours before the scheduled 3 p.m. flight.

As the jumbo jet lifted off, the controller in the tower realized that something was wrong. In a matter of seconds, the left turbofan engine of the great airplane had broken loose of its moorings. The engine fell off onto the runway and fuel was pouring out of the hole where the engine should have been.

The jet climbed a few hundred feet before it turned perpendicular to the ground and fell in an abandoned airfield near a trailer park in Elk Grove Village. The explosion of the plane allowed no chance of survival for any of the passengers or crew.

Flames from the wreckage were seen as far away as eight miles and at least one home in the trailer park burned up as well. Had the plane not disintegrated as quickly as it did, more damage to the mobile homes would have occurred.

The flames were so intense that rescue workers could not get near the wreckage for an hour. When they could finally move in, all that remained for them to do was the ghoulish task of marking the charred bodies and unidentified remains. Colored markers on wooden stakes dotted the field to show where bodies lay among all that remained of the DC-10.

The National Transportation Safety Board sent a team to investigate the crash—not the first of a McDonnell Douglas DC-10. As a result of the crash and the investigation which followed, all DC-10's were grounded in the

The DC-10, which was en route to Los Angeles from Chicago's O'Hare Airport, climbed a few hundred feet before it crashed in an abandoned airfield near a trailer park in Elk Grove Village.

United States and declared unsafe to fly. But that was after the fact. Nothing could change the tragedy which occurred at O'Hare Airport at the start of that Memorial Day weekend.

Debris covered the runway after the DC-10 crash. The forklift in the background removed the engine which fell from the plane onto the runway.

Although firemen battled the flames, the explosion of the plane allowed no chance of survival for any of the passengers or crew.

Rescue workers shown here marked the charred bodies and unidentified remains of the crash victims with colored markers on wooden stakes.

POLISH IL-62 EXPLODES: U.S. LOSES AMATEUR BOXING TEAM

March 14, 1980

Polish Airlines Flight 007 was delayed from takeoff in New York City for two hours due to a severe snowstorm. The jetliner was a Polish IL-62 made in the Soviet Union and on this particular flight had 77 passengers and 10 crew members aboard.

Although the flight left New York during bad weather conditions, when it completed its nonstop trip to Warsaw, the weather was clear and landing conditions were good.

Aboard the flight were 14 members of the U.S. amateur boxing team which planned to fight in Krakow and Katowice against the Poles. Also included on the passenger list was the team's coach, Thomas "Sarge" Johnson, aged 58, and the man responsible for training the U.S. boxers who had won five gold medals at the 1976 Olympics in Montreal.

The airplane had made a satisfactory ocean crossing and was nearing Warsaw's Okecie Airport when a sudden explosion shook the huge airliner. The plane plummeted into the earthworks at a 19th-century fort located just two miles from the airport. The explosion and ensuing crash killed all of the 77 passengers aboard as well as the 10 members of the crew.

Among those killed were 23-year-old Lemuel Steeples of St. Louis, the top-ranking American in the light-welterweight class. Andre McCoy, a light heavyweight from New Bedford, Massachusetts, also died in the crash. Both of these young men were considered contenders for the U.S. Summer Olympics team.

Boxing devotees as well as the entire nation mourned the death of these young men in one of the worst disasters to befall a United States sporting team. Other tragic air accidents had befallen American athletes in the past but the deaths of these boxers brought tears to the eyes of grown men.

The air crash which tore apart the huge Polish IL-62 also took a tremendous toll of American amateur boxing ranks.

One talented heavyweight might have said that fate intervened in his behalf. Twenty-five-year-old Jimmy Clark of Coatesville, Pennsylvania was snowbound by the same storm which had delayed the Polish jet. Because he was not able to leave Philadelphia to get to New York, he was not aboard Flight 007. He mourned the deaths of his friends, however, as did the rest of the sporting world both in the United States and abroad.

Flag-draped caskets of Americans killed in the Polish jetliner crash near Warsaw are lined up at Andrews Air Force Base, Maryland. All those onboard the plane were killed in the crash, including 14 members of the U.S. amateur boxing team.